AF732267

# Faith 4 Life

## Senior High Bible Study Series

# Sharing Your Faith

Group
Loveland, Colorado

## Group's R.E.A.L. Guarantee to you:

This Group resource incorporates our R.E.A.L. approach to ministry—one that encourages long-term retention and life transformation. It's ministry that's:

**Relational**
Because learner-to-learner interaction enhances learning and builds Christian friendships.

**Experiential**
Because what learners experience through discussion and action sticks with them up to 9 times longer than what they simply hear or read.

**Applicable**
Because the aim of Christian education is to equip learners to be both hearers and doers of God's Word.

**Learner-based**
Because learners understand and retain more when the learning process takes into consideration how they learn best.

Faith 4 Life
SENIOR HIGH BIBLE STUDY SERIES

# Sharing Your Faith



Visit our Web site: **www.grouppublishing.com**

**Credits**
Contributing Authors: Rick Lawrence, Erin McKay, Pamela J. Shoup, and Jane Vogel
Editor: Amy Simpson
Creative Development Editor: Dave Thornton
Chief Creative Officer: Joani Schultz
Copy Editor: Janis Sampson
Art Director: Sharon Anderson
Print Production Artist: Stephen Beer
Cover Art Director/Designer: Jeff A. Storm
Cover Photographer: Daniel Treat
Production Manager: DeAnne Lear



ISBN 0-7644-2466-1

10 9 8 7 6 5 4 3 2 1 12 11 10 09 08 07 06 05 04 03

Printed in the United States of America.

# Contents

INTRODUCTION

# Sharing Your Faith

Sharing your faith in Christ doesn't just mean telling someone how to become a Christian. It can also mean asking God to give you the strength to live a life that would draw someone to him. It means caring for people's needs and leaning on God to give you the right words at the right time. And it means letting the Holy Spirit strengthen you when you've done all you can.

The first study in this book will help teenagers identify their own faith stories and examine the impact God has had on their lives. Teenagers will learn how to find God's truth in their stories and how to share their own stories with others in practical, natural ways.

***It means caring for people's needs and leaning on God to give you the right words at the right time.***

In the second study, teenagers will experience ways they can act as God's instruments through their expressions of joy in Christ. This study will help teenagers realize that they don't always have to "do something" to share their faith with others—sometimes simply living their lives with pure Christian joy is the greatest possible way of sharing faith.

The third study in this book will give teenagers a deeper awareness of global missions while encouraging them to find their own mission fields, whether overseas or in their own hometowns. Teenagers will understand that the Holy Spirit gives them the power and confidence they need to share Christ with the world.

The fourth study focuses on the issue of persecution because of faith. Teenagers will be motivated to take action in spite of the risk of persecution and ostracism, and they'll be encouraged by the promise of God's blessings upon those who suffer in his name.

Teenagers need to know that sharing their faith with others isn't just a religious duty. When God opens teenagers' hearts to help them see all that he's done for them, sharing their faith with others will be a natural outward expression of their lives as Christians. And their lives will change as they demonstrate their faith through their words and their actions.

# Senior High Bible Study Series

Faith 4 Life: Senior High Bible Study Series helps teenagers take a Bible-based approach to faith and life issues. Each book in the series contains these important elements:

- ***Life application of Bible truth***
  Faith 4 Life studies help teenagers understand what the Bible says and then apply that truth to their lives.
- ***A relevant topic***
  Each Faith 4 Life book focuses on one main topic, with four studies to give your students a thorough understanding of how the Bible relates to that topic. These topics were chosen by youth leaders as the ones most relevant for senior high students.
- ***One point***
  Each study makes one point, centering on that one theme to make sure students really understand the important truth it conveys. This point is stated upfront and throughout the study.
- ***Simplicity***
  The studies are easy to use. Each contains a "Before the Study" box that outlines any advance preparation required. Each study also contains a "Study at a Glance" chart so you can quickly and easily see what supplies you'll need and what each study will involve.
- ***Action and interaction***
  Each study relies on experiential learning to help students learn what God's Word has to say. Teenagers discuss and debrief their experiences in large groups, small groups, and individual reflection.
- ***Reproducible handouts***
  Faith 4 Life books include reproducible handouts for students. No need for student books!
- ***Tips, tips, and more tips***
  Faith 4 Life studies are full of "FYI" tips for the teacher, providing extra ideas, insights into young people, and hints for making the studies go smoothly.
- ***Flexibility***
  Faith 4 Life studies include optional activities and bonus activities. Use a study as it's written, or use these options to create the study that works best for your group.
- ***Follow-up ideas***
  At the end of each book, you'll find a section called "Changed 4 Life." This section provides ideas for following up with your students to make sure the studies stick with them.

Use Faith 4 Life studies to show your teenagers how the Bible is relevant to their lives. Help them see that God can invade every area of their lives and change them in ways they can only imagine. Encourage your students to go deeper into faith—faith that will sustain them for life! Faith 4 Life, forever!

# WHAT'S YOUR STORY?

Let's say a visitor walks into your youth meeting, but instead of a normal greeting like "What's up?" or "How's it goin'?" he says, "What's your story? Why are you really here?"

What would your group members say? Do they have stories to tell about their relationships with God? And if they do, do they know how to tell them?

What if one of your group members spoke out and said, "My story is about grace—how much I've needed it and how often God has offered it to me. My story is about trying to make life work on my own, but ending up lost, isolated, lonely, and afraid. And my story is about how, in the middle of that darkness, God loved me and offered to be the co-author of my life. Now I'm learning that God doesn't want to write my story for me—he wants to write it with me. And as we create together, I'm learning that my story can actually offer hope and truth to others. That's my story. Would you like to hear more?"

Your teenagers each have a story to tell—one that God has helped write. Others need to hear those stories—people who need hope but can't find it. This study will help your teenagers find God's grace in their stories, then tell their stories to those around them.

# THE POINT

**You have to know your story before you can share it.**

# SCRIPTURE SOURCE

**2 Kings 22–23**
King Josiah reminds God's people of God's role in their story.

**Philippians 3:2-11**
Paul tells how God "rewrote" his life's story—saving him from pride and giving him new life.

# THE STUDY AT A GLANCE

## #1 For Starters
**15-20 Minutes**

**■ SPLATTERED STORIES**

**What students will do:**
*Create a personalized space on the floor and then share something about themselves.*

SUPPLIES:
- ❑ newsprint
- ❑ tape
- ❑ pens
- ❑ colored markers
- ❑ old magazines
- ❑ glue
- ❑ scissors

**■ OPTIONAL ACTIVITY**
**15-20 Minutes**

**What students will do:**
*Create a personalized space on the floor and write stories about their lives.*

SUPPLIES:
- ❑ paper
- ❑ "Splattered Stories" supplies

## #2 Bible Truth
**20-25 Minutes**

**■ A TALE OF TWO MEN**

**What students will do:**
*Explore the lives of two men in the Bible whose stories were powerfully impacted by God.*

SUPPLIES:
- ❑ Bibles
- ❑ newsprint
- ❑ tape
- ❑ markers

## #3 Life Application
**10-15 Minutes**

**■ GIVE YOUR LIFE AWAY**

**What students will do:**
*Create personal symbols that represent God's impact on their stories and then choose ways to use the symbols in telling their stories.*

SUPPLIES:
- ❑ markers
- ❑ pens

## BEFORE THE STUDY

Move the furniture to the sides of your meeting room, and cover the floor with newsprint (you may want to tape the newsprint to the floor in spots to keep it from shifting). Gather old magazines, colored markers, pens, glue, and scissors, and pile them together in the center of the room. Be prepared to tell group members a story of how God has changed your life.

# FOR STARTERS

**15 to 20 minutes**

## SPLATTERED STORIES

As teenagers enter your meeting room, have them remove their shoes. Then have teenagers spread out around the room and each create his or her own "personal space" on the floor by drawing a shape (a circle, square, letter outline, or whatever) on the newsprint. The shape should be big enough to sit in. Ask teenagers to decorate their shapes however they'd like (point them to the supply pile for decoration ideas).

When teenagers finish, form groups of three by having teenagers get together with two other people whose shapes are located close to theirs. Have trios each draw a circle in the space between their three shapes, then sit down around the circle.

**Say: Show your two partners your personal space design, then draw a pathway from your shape to the circle you just created.**

Once trios finish this task, **say:**

**Now complete the following statement about each of your partners by writing inside the pathway that leads from your personal space to the circle. Here's the statement: "**[Name]**, based on how you've decorated your personal space, I think you're a person who..."**

When trios have finished, **say:**

**Now look at what your group members wrote about you. Tell them whether they're right or wrong about you and why.**

After a few minutes, ask teenagers to tell what they learned about their group members. Then **ask:**

- **How did it feel to have others draw conclusions about you with very little information?**

- How did it feel when they were right? wrong?
- How did you feel when you gave someone in your group feedback and that person disagreed with your conclusions? agreed?
- How are all these feelings like the way you feel when you're relating with people at school, home, work, or church?

**Say:** **Tell your partners something you'd like them to know about you. When you've finished, write in the circle one thing you liked about what your partners shared.**

Then **say:**

**Each of us has a story to tell about who we are. Often the people around us, even our closest friends, don't understand us because we're not always that good at telling our own stories. Today we'll investigate our own stories and the stories of the people around us and learn how we can help others by sharing God's impact on our lives. Remember this: You have to know your story before you can share it with others. To discover more about how to do this, let's explore how God deeply impacted the stories of two men and what happened because of his impact.**

THE POINT

## OPTIONAL ACTIVITY

**15 to 20 minutes**

Instead of the "Splattered Stories" activity, try this one if you want to make this study deeper and more personal for your students.

As teenagers enter your meeting room, have them remove their shoes. Then have teenagers spread out around the room and each create his or her own "personal space" on the floor by drawing a shape (a circle, square, letter outline, or whatever) on the newsprint. The shape should be big enough to sit in. Ask teenagers to decorate their shapes however they'd like (point them to the supply pile for decoration ideas).

Ask teenagers to find partners. Have pairs draw a pathway between their personal spaces. Then **say:**

**Inside your personal space, write a short story about God's influence in your life. For example, you could write about a time when...**

- **things seemed bleak, but God somehow gave you hope.**
- **you were hurt and confused because God didn't act the way you expected him to.**
- **you felt close to God.**
- **you felt far away from God.**
- **you felt like standing up for God.**
- **you felt like you really needed God in your life.**

After a few minutes, **say:**

**Now I'd like you to talk to your partner about what you wrote. Be sure you tell your partner something you learned about yourself because of this life experience.**

After partners share, have them **discuss** these questions:

- **Was it easy to think of some way God has impacted your story? Why or why not?**
- **What's most difficult about telling someone else about God's impact on your life?**
- **If your school friends knew about God's impact on you, how would that affect them?**
- **What does it mean to share your faith with someone?**

**Say: Even though God has co-authored our stories, it's easy to "edit out" his impact on us when we're telling our stories to others. That's why it's important to be prepared to talk with others about God's role in our lives. Today we'll investigate**

**our own stories and the stories of the people around us and learn how we can help others by sharing God's impact on our lives. Remember this: You have to know your story before you can share it with others. To discover more about how to do this, let's explore how God deeply impacted the stories of two men and what happened because of his impact.**

THE POINT

*FYI

What about teenagers who say they're Christians but have no evident relationship with Christ? If teenagers claim God has no impact on their lives, consider calling them aside and lovingly confronting them with these difficult questions:

- What does being a Christian mean to you?
- The Bible teaches that being a Christian means receiving God's forgiveness for our sins, then following Jesus every day. Do you think this is true? Why or why not?
- If what the Bible teaches is true, why would it be important for a follower of Jesus to have an ongoing, daily relationship with him?
- Do you want an ongoing, daily relationship with Jesus? Why or why not?

If teenagers express interest in a personal relationship with Jesus, pray with them right there, asking God to guide them into a personal relationship with him.

# BIBLE TRUTH

20 to 25 minutes

*FYI

The Josiah Scripture passage is longer than usual—two complete chapters. You may want to have the Josiah group pick a number of students to read this passage aloud.

## A TALE OF TWO MEN

At opposite ends of your meeting area, draw circles on the newsprint, and write in one the name "Paul" and in the other the name "Josiah." Then **say:**

**Imagine that marriage and a family will one day be a part of your story. Imagine that you and your spouse are pregnant with a son, and you have just these two names to choose from—which one would you pick to name your son? Once you decide, draw a pathway to the circle that represents your choice and sit near it.**

Once teenagers have gathered by the two circles, give each group a Bible and ask each group to pick a reader. Then **say:**

**In a moment I'll assign each reader a Bible passage to read aloud. As you listen to the passage, think about how you'd answer these two questions: "How did God impact this person's story?" and "Why did this person respond to God the way he did?"**

Tell the Josiah group reader to read aloud 2 Kings 22–23. Have the Paul group reader read aloud Philippians 3:2-11. While the readers are reading, write the two questions on newsprint and tape the newsprint to the wall.

When both readers finish, have groups discuss the two questions you wrote on the newsprint. Then have each group appoint a reporter to tell what the group learned about its biblical character. After the reporters share, tell teenagers your own story of how God has changed your life. Then call everyone together and **ask:**

- **How have these stories—mine, Josiah's, and Paul's—impacted you?**
- **How can your story impact others for Christ?**

Have teenagers look around the room at the newsprint "network" they've created. **Ask:**

- **How is creating these pathways on the newsprint like sharing our stories with others in real life?**
- **What would happen to you if you never shared your story with anyone?**

**Say: You have to know your story before you can share it. Now let's learn more about ways you can share your story with others.** THE POINT

# LIFE APPLICATION

**10 to 15 minutes**

## GIVE YOUR LIFE AWAY

**Say: We've begun to see God's impact on others' stories and our own. But how can we let others know the good news that God loves us and wants to be a co-author with us in creating our life stories? In your personal space, I'd like you to create a symbol or drawing that represents God's impact on your life's story. Then we'll discuss ways you can use your symbol or drawing to tell your story. But before we begin, let's ask our "co-author" to help us share our stories with the people around us.**

Open the prayer time by asking God to show teenagers how he has impacted their lives, then invite teenagers to express their own prayers to God, either silently or aloud.

After the prayer time, pile colored markers in the center of your room for teenagers to use in creating their symbols. When teenagers finish, have two or three young people explain their symbols' meanings to the group.

Then **say:**

**To close, I'd like each of you to tear your symbol out of your personal space, then write on the back one way you can use your symbol to tell others about God's impact on your life. For example, you could draw your symbol on all your school notebooks, then use it as an opportunity to share your story with friends at school.**

When teenagers have finished, **say:**

**I challenge you to follow through with your idea this week. Now that you know something of your story, you can share it with others!** THE POINT

### *FYI

Josiah stands out in Old Testament history as a passionate reformer and humble leader.

Josiah began his journey as a leader when he was only eight years old. Before Josiah became king, Judah had grown corrupt with foreign, idolatrous influences. For more than fifty years, idol worship had replaced the law of Moses, and immorality was rampant. In fact, the people of Judah so ignored God in their daily lives that Josiah didn't even know what God expected of his people. When workers restoring the Temple in Jerusalem discovered a copy of God's laws, Josiah read them and grieved that the people had strayed so far from God's design for them.

When Josiah was just sixteen, he stopped practicing the traditional idol worship of the people and searched for ways to honor God in his life. Then when he was twenty, he decided to vigorously purge idolatry from Judah. He ordered that altars, statues, and icons of pagan gods be destroyed. He banished prostitutes from the Temple, banned child sacrifices, and removed idolatrous religious leaders from office. At the same time, he repopularized the reading of God's laws and personally pledged to follow them with all his heart.

# JOY OF THE LORD

Pop quiz: Who would you rather be like, Tigger or Eeyore?

OK, if that's too simplistic, think of this: Who was more attractive to the public: Princess Diana or Prince Charles?

As the many outpourings of emotion over the princess's death made clear, the charm of "the people's princess" lay in more than her physical beauty and her glamorous lifestyle. Diana won hearts by her obvious love of life, even when life was handing her lemons. She had an inner glow that drew people as a candle draws moths to its light.

If Diana's inner joy could have that effect on people, think what an impact the real thing could make! Think what an attraction the joy of the Lord would have if people were only able to see it clearly in our lives!

Use this lesson to help teenagers see that they don't always have to *do* something to share their faith; sometimes the way they live their lives is the strongest witness. Help teenagers discover that when non-Christians see the amazing life transformations that come when people live lives of true joy in Christ, they will want to find out how they can live their lives the same way.

Equip your students to be more than just "a candle in the wind"; challenge them to be light to the world.

# THE POINT

**God can reach others through you.**

# SCRIPTURE SOURCE

## Matthew 5:13-16

The expression of Christ in our lives can make our faith attractive to other people.

## 1 Peter 1:3-9

Through Christ, we have a joy that cannot be explained even when circumstances make us sad.

# THE STUDY AT A GLANCE

## #1 For Starters

**15-20 Minutes**

### ■ NOTHIN' LIKE THE REAL THING

**What students will do:**
*Do a taste test to see if they can tell the real thing from the imitation, then discuss the difference between expressing true joy and just faking it.*

SUPPLIES:
- ❑ Bibles
- ❑ samples of food and beverages
- ❑ scissors
- ❑ paper
- ❑ pens
- ❑ "ballot" boxes
- ❑ markers
- ❑ white board

## #2 Bible Truth

**20-25 Minutes**

### ■ DRAWN TO THE LIGHT

**What students will do:**
*Make life-size examples of joyful and crabby Christians, then reflect on how well they exhibit true joy.*

SUPPLIES:
- ❑ Bibles
- ❑ long sheets of newsprint
- ❑ markers
- ❑ magazines
- ❑ scissors
- ❑ glue sticks

## #3 Life Application

**10-15 Minutes**

### ■ GETTING DOWN TO BUSINESS

**What students will do:**
*Make magnetized business cards to remind them of practical ways to demonstrate the joy of the Lord.*

SUPPLIES:
- ❑ Bible
- ❑ paper
- ❑ markers
- ❑ newsprint
- ❑ scissors
- ❑ magnets

### ■ OPTIONAL ACTIVITY

**10-15 Minutes**

**What students will do:**
*Come up with plans to increase joy in their lives by spending time in Christ's presence and getting to know Jesus better.*

SUPPLIES:
- ❑ paper
- ❑ pens

## BEFORE THE STUDY

Set up one or more taste tests—set out food or beverage samples in pairs, with each pair consisting of the real thing and an imitation (for example, you might use a name-brand cola and a generic cola, real chocolate chips and chocolate-flavored baking morsels, and real ice cream and frozen nondairy dessert). Remove all labels that would indicate which sample is the real thing and which is the imitation. Label each sample in a pair either "A" or "B" (making sure that in some pairs the imitation is A and in some it is B so that teenagers don't find a pattern), and provide pens and slips of paper for teenagers to use as ballots. Place a box or a paper bag by each pair of samples for teenagers to put their completed ballots in.

You'll need magnets that are the size of a business card and are self-adhesive for the "Getting Down to Business" activity. These are available at office supply stores; they're made for business people to attach to the back of their business cards.

*FYI

Christian joy is more than just feeling happy. Happiness is usually a response to external circumstances: getting good grades on final exams, enjoying an evening out with friends, or having a "good hair day." True joy, however, goes deeper than circumstances. As 1 Peter 1:3-5 shows, Christian joy is founded on the reality of our new life in Christ, our status as members of God's own family, and our hope that stretches beyond the present into eternity. This is not to say that joy is reserved for some distant time in the sweet by-and-by, however. Because of our love and our faith now, we can also experience deep joy now (see 1 Peter 1:8), even when external circumstances are unpleasant.

# FOR STARTERS

**15 to 20 minutes**

## NOTHIN' LIKE THE REAL THING

As teenagers arrive, conduct a taste test by letting them taste the samples you set out before the study. For each pair of samples, instruct teenagers to write the letter of the sample that they think is the real thing on a slip of paper and put it in the ballot box or paper bag by that pair of samples.

When everyone has had a chance to sample and vote, unveil the identities of the samples and see whether the teenagers were able to tell the difference. (For the discussion that follows, it doesn't matter whether teenagers guessed right or wrong.) **Ask:**

- **How could you tell the real thing from the imitation?**
- **Why do the imitations want to pass themselves off as the real thing?**
- **Today we're going to talk about Christian joy. Can you think of ways people try to fake joy? Explain.**
- **How might you be able to tell fake joy from the real thing?**

**Say: We talk a lot about joy. Let's take a better look at what true joy really is.**

Have students form groups of four. Hand out Bibles, paper, and pens.

**Say: In your foursome, read 1 Peter 1:3-9 and write a definition of true joy based on that passage.**

As foursomes finish their definitions, **say:**

**Stay in your group of four, and think about people you know who are truly joyful Christians. Then have each person in your group tell the rest of the foursome about specific ways someone you know has exhibited true joy.**

After a few minutes, have each foursome share its definition of joy with the whole group and then share one or more of the "true joy" stories. As teenagers share their ideas, write the definitions on a white board or a sheet of newsprint. Listen for qualities in the people described, and write those down as well.

When every foursome has had a chance to report, **ask:**

- **What do you see as the relationship between suffering and joy?**
- **When is it hard for you to be joyful?**
- **How is it that some people can be joyful even in hard times?**
- **What impact do you think joy has on others? For example, how could your joy affect people who see your joy even in hard times?**
- **How might your joy enable God to reach others through you?**

THE POINT

*FYI

If you think teenagers may have difficulty thinking of examples, be ready with an example of your own that you can share.

*FYI

As teenagers share stories about people who show true joy in their lives, they may not know exactly why they have chosen those people as examples. You can help deepen their understanding by identifying *actions* (these may be things such as listening to others, expressing faith or thankfulness even in a crisis, smiling a lot, or tackling tough jobs with energy and enthusiasm) and *attitudes* (these may be things such as a positive outlook, inner peace, or confidence) that teenagers mention in their descriptions of joyful people they know.

*NOTES

# BIBLE TRUTH

20 to 25 minutes

## DRAWN TO THE LIGHT

Have teenagers stay in their same groups of four. Give foursomes long sheets of newsprint, magazines, scissors, markers, and glue sticks. Assign half of the groups to make life-size "Joyful Christians" and the other half to make "Crabby Christians." Suggest each group trace around a person who's lying on the paper, cut out various features from magazines to glue onto the outline, and then add its own artwork.

**Say: The figure you create should be more than just a smiling or a frowning person. It should include things representative of positive or negative attitudes associated with Christians. For example, Crabby Christian might have a speech balloon around magazine pictures of a happy couple and a sports car—both crossed out. Next to the pictures inside the speech balloon might be the words "Thou shalt not engage in public displays of affection" and "Thou shalt not drive fast cars."**

After foursomes have made their figures, let them display and explain them. Then have teenagers read Matthew 5:14-16 in their foursomes and **discuss** these questions:

- **How is a joyful Christian like a city on a hill?**
- **What are some of the things about a joyful Christian that make his or her faith attractive to others?**
- **Who do you know that is a joyful Christian? How does that person's joy show?**
- **Do you consider yourself a joyful Christian?**

*FYI

When you debrief the "Drawn to the Light" activity, address ways we as Christians can look at things we should not do—such as engaging in drunkenness or sexual promiscuity—in a positive light. For example, you might point out that we don't need alcohol to have fun or that we don't need to barter our bodies to feel accepted. Let teenagers know two things: (1) We should never sacrifice moral standards just because we think it will make us more appealing as we share our faith with others; and (2) we do not need to present the challenges of the Christian life in a negative light. We can take a stand on moral issues without being Crabby Christians.

Refer to the definitions of joy and the qualities of a joyful Christian that you compiled in the previous activity as teenagers reflect on whether their lives demonstrate true joy.

Have teenagers form pairs. **Say:**

**Share with your partner one area in your life in which you want to develop or show more joy. For example, you might want to become more joyful in your relationships with your family, or you might want to be able to find more joy in your role as a student. After you've each shared those areas, don't tell your partner what he or she ought to do to be more joyful! Instead of giving advice, spend a few minutes praying for your partner and the area he or she shared.**

**Say: God can reach others through you. In fact, he probably already does. Share with your partner one way that you see the joy of the Lord in his or her life. Be as specific as you can. For example, your partner might be someone who tries to have a smile for everyone. That's one way of reaching out. Or maybe you've seen your partner deal with a disappointment or an inconvenience without losing his or her cool. That's evidence of Christian joy.**

THE POINT

*NOTES

# LIFE APPLICATION

10 to 15 minutes

## GETTING DOWN TO BUSINESS

Read Matthew 5:14-16 aloud again, and **say:**

> **God can reach others through you. Often when we think about reaching others for God, we think about saying the right things. And it's important to be able to talk about our faith. But did you notice that this passage doesn't talk at all about what we say, just about what we do? Ask:**

THE POINT

- **What are some things you could do to show your joy?**
- **How might those actions make your faith attractive to other people?**
- **How do you feel about the idea that your attitudes and actions can be as important a part of your faith sharing as what you say?**

Hand out paper, markers, and self-adhesive business-card-sized magnets. **Say:**

> **It's our business as Christians to live as lights—people whose joy makes the Christian faith attractive. Ask:**

- **What are some specific ways we could show our joy this week?**

Compile a list of ideas on newsprint, then have each person choose one idea to implement this week. Have teenagers each make a "business card" with an idea, a logo, or a slogan reminding them of the idea. Have teenagers attach their business cards to the magnets, and urge them to stick their magnets in their school lockers where they'll see them and be reminded every day.

Close the meeting with this reminder:

THE POINT

> **God can reach others through you! Let your light shine so that others will be drawn to Jesus, the light of the world.**

## OPTIONAL ACTIVITY

10 to 15 minutes

Instead of the "Getting Down to Business" activity, try this optional activity to spark spiritual growth in your students.

Read Matthew 5:14-16 aloud again, and **say:**

> **God can reach others through you. The best way to exhibit joy to others is to experience joy in knowing Christ. And the best way to do that is simply to spend time in his presence, getting to know him better.**

THE POINT

**Ask:**
- **What are some different ways we can spend time in Christ's presence?**
- **What are some different ways we can get to know Jesus better?**

**Say: I'd like to encourage each of you to construct a plan for carrying out one of these things over the next month or so.**

Give students paper and pens. Ask each person to find some space in the room, away from other people and distractions. Spend a few minutes in silence or with quiet music playing in the background. Encourage students to spend the time with God, asking him to show them a commitment they can make to spend time in Christ's presence or to get to know Jesus better over the next month or so.

After a few minutes, encourage teenagers to write out their plans.

**Say: Take your paper with you, and put it in a place where it will remind you to carry out your plan. Then watch how the joy of the Lord will begin to overflow from your life.**

### *FYI

It's tempting—perhaps especially for self-conscious teenagers who don't want to risk embarrassing themselves—to limit our faith sharing to the nonverbal. It's easy to rationalize that if actions speak louder than words, then we don't really ever have to say the words.

God, of course, doesn't see it quite this way. Scripture makes it clear that Christians are to share their faith through both word and action. Certainly our lifestyles are to be joyful as they demonstrate what Lord we serve. But we are also to be salt and light (as this passage in Matthew reminds us) in what we say. Colossians 4:3-6 uses the same salt imagery that we see in Matthew, but here it is very clear that being salt includes speaking the gospel to unbelievers: "Make the most of your chances to tell others the Good News" (Colossians 4:5a, The Living Bible).

The verbal and nonverbal sharing of our faith go hand in hand. The joy that people see in our lives backs up the words we speak.

*FYI

A terrific way for your group to let God use them to reach others is by hosting an event for their non-Christian friends. This event can be as simple or as involved as your resources permit, but it should include certain things:

- It should be fun. While fun is not the same as joy, it certainly helps non-Christians see that the Christian life is not all gloom and doom!
- It should be nonthreatening. Using church jargon, expecting teenagers to know where to look in the Bible or songbook, and even telling teenagers to meet in the "narthex" can all be intimidating to those who don't have much experience with church life.
- It should include a clear presentation of the gospel. After all, it isn't outreach if you don't reach out, is it? Such a presentation need not be long or heavy-handed, and you don't have to call for a public commitment; but you do need to be sure that the teenagers who come have a chance to discover the source of true joy!

# SEND ME!

Today hundreds of thousands of missionaries have received the call to work around the globe to spread the message of the gospel to non-Christians. And billions still need to be reached by the message. Mission work is a selfless job which often requires hardship, suffering, and sometimes even death. Not an attractive-sounding career choice for a teenager.

But teenagers' youthful idealism—a desire to change the world (in a few weeks or less)—gives them a natural affinity toward mission work. Get teenagers involved in missions close to home or across the world to help them experience true Christian fellowship, and many will have life-changing experiences. Every person may not feel the call to enter international missions. But all people have places where they can share Christ—with friends and in their own communities, where the need may be as great as somewhere across an ocean.

The power to share Christ comes from the Holy Spirit as Jesus told his disciples in Acts 1:8a: "You will receive power when the Holy Spirit comes on you; and you will be my witnesses." Through this study your teenagers will have the opportunity to explore missions; identify their own call to share their faith; and ask themselves, "What can I do to bring Christ's message to the world?"

# THE POINT

**The world needs Jesus.**

# SCRIPTURE SOURCE

### Matthew 25:31-46

Jesus teaches about those who will inherit the kingdom of heaven.

### Matthew 28:18-20

Christ appears to his eleven disciples and instructs them to make disciples of all nations.

### Mark 1:17

As Jesus calls his disciples, he promises to make them "fishers of men."

### Acts 1:8

The resurrected Christ promises the apostles they will receive power to share faith when the Holy Spirit comes upon them.

### Ephesians 6:19

Paul prays for the gift of words to help him spread the gospel fearlessly.

# THE STUDY AT A GLANCE

## #1 For Starters

**10-15 Minutes**

**■ FISHERS OF MEN**

**What students will do:**
*Explore the idea of being called to mission work.*

SUPPLIES:
- ❑ Bible
- ❑ paper
- ❑ scissors
- ❑ pen

## #2 Bible Truth

**25-30 Minutes**

**■ CAST THE NET**

**What students will do:**
*Create fictional countries, identify missionary needs, pray for unreached people, and identify how they can support foreign missions.*

SUPPLIES:
- ❑ Bibles
- ❑ poster board
- ❑ markers
- ❑ newsprint

## #3 Life Application

**10-15 Minutes**

**■ POWER FROM THE SPIRIT**

**What students will do:**
*Reflect on their own calls to missions and commit to service.*

SUPPLIES:
- ❑ Bibles
- ❑ matches
- ❑ candles
- ❑ pens
- ❑ candleholders
- ❑ journals or paper

**■ OPTIONAL ACTIVITY**

**10-15 Minutes**

**What students will do:**
*Identify local mission needs and be challenged to reach outside their comfort zones.*

SUPPLIES:
- ❑ newsprint
- ❑ marker

## BEFORE THE STUDY

Prepare four "mission slips" on different slips of paper for the "Fishers of Men" activity. The four different slips should read "living in a foreign country"; "performing, singing, or acting"; "teaching or practicing medicine"; and "bringing people to Christ."

# FOR STARTERS

10 to 15 minutes

## FISHERS OF MEN

As teenagers arrive, choose four volunteers, take them aside, and tell them that the goal in the opening activity is for each of them to get the most people to join his or her group. Have each volunteer choose one of the mission slips you prepared before the study. Explain that volunteers are to entice other students to join their groups based on the students' interests and the leader's persuasiveness. For example, leaders might promote the benefits of joining their groups by telling about the excitement of living overseas, opportunities to use various talents, a life dedicated to helping others, or a life dedicated to spreading God's Word.

Once everyone has arrived, welcome teenagers and **say:**

**Let's start off today with an activity to get everybody up and moving around. I've selected four people who each have a mission to accomplish. Listen to what they have to say, and decide which mission you would like to be a part of.**

Allow about a minute for groups to form, then have teenagers sit down with their groups. If any leader was unable to attract followers, have him or her sit with another group. **Ask:**

- **Leaders, how did you get people to join your group?**
- **Followers, why did you choose the area of need that you chose?**
- **Leaders, why couldn't some of you get many followers?**
- **Followers, did your leader offer promises he or she couldn't fulfill? Explain.**
- **Does God ever offer promises he can't fulfill? Explain.**

***FYI**

You may adjust the number of volunteers according to the size of your group. [Plan on one volunteer for every four students.] Reduce or expand the number of mission slips as needed. You might choose students who are natural leaders so each leader will attract at least one follower.

**Say: I call this activity "Fishers of Men," based on Mark 1:17, since you all "fished" for followers for your missions.** Have a volunteer read Mark 1:17 aloud. **Say: Modern-day fishers of men are missionaries, and today we're going to explore mission work at home and throughout the world because the world needs Jesus. The message spread by missions is God's truth. God is always true to his promises and his Word, and that's what we as Christians need to tell the world.**

THE POINT

**The disciples received a "call" from Jesus to become his followers. Today you'll have a chance to explore your own thoughts and feelings about mission work and perhaps determine whether God might want you to serve him in that way.** Have teenagers **discuss** the following questions in their groups:

- **How might you know if God wants you to do mission work?**
- **How might you determine an area of need that you could meet?**
- **What various talents, knowledge, or education would be helpful in mission work?**

Allow groups to share some of their answers, then **say:**

**Singing and performing, traveling to foreign countries, spreading the Word of God, or teaching and doing medical work are some of the jobs done by missionaries as they use the truth of God's Word to gather followers for Jesus. Let's take a closer look at mission work.**

*FYI

If any groups are struggling for ideas, give them some of these suggestions: building churches or houses, establishing schools, starting Bible studies, training native missionaries and pastors, building water systems, responding to medical and health needs, easing suffering caused by war or natural disasters, translating or interpreting the local language, providing Bibles in native languages, or communicating the gospel through music and drama as well as through one-on-one sharing.

# BIBLE TRUTH

25 to 30 minutes

## CAST THE NET

Have teenagers divide into groups of four to six (or remain in their groups from the previous activity), and have members of each group sit together on the floor. Give each group a sheet of poster board, a marker, and a Bible.

**Say: On your poster board, draw a shape of a fictional country. Make up a name and a fictional religion for your country, and write them on the poster board.**

Give teenagers a few minutes to complete the task, then **say:**

**Now you are missionaries who are going to bring Christianity to this country because the world needs Jesus. On your poster board, list the needs the people in your country might have that missionaries could respond to. I'll come around and give you some ideas if you need help.** THE POINT

After a few minutes, have each group share its poster with the entire group. They may elaborate on any interesting "facts" about their country, its religion, or its mission needs. Then have each group read Matthew 25:31-46 together and **discuss** these questions:

- **How do your lists of mission needs correspond with the directives Jesus gave in this Scripture passage?**
- **How can you as a missionary share your faith in all that you do?**
- **When you as a missionary serve others, who are you really serving? Explain.**

**Say: You've come up with some real needs for your fictional countries. When you serve God's people, you are serving God. You can meet the world's need for Jesus.** THE POINT

**In spite of the efforts of nearly half a million missionaries in foreign countries, there are still people Christians call unreached. Unreached people are those who misunderstand or have no knowledge of Christ or the gospel. Most of these people don't know about Christ because there are no active Christians who speak their languages to share the Word of God in ways they can accept and understand within their cultures. In other words, there are no Christian movements in their countries large enough to bring people to Christ.**

**Some churches "adopt" groups of unreached people and try to help mission efforts in those countries. Other Christians make a point of praying for certain groups of unreached people.**

**One of these groups of unreached people is the Minang people group in West Sumatra, which is part of Indonesia. The Minang believe that Christians worship three gods: god the father, god the son, and god the mother. Of the four million Minang people in West Sumatra, there are less than fifty Christians.**

**Another unreached people is the Tu group of China. They are Buddhists, and there are no known Christians among their nearly two hundred thousand people. It is estimated that 86 percent of the Tu people have never even heard the name Jesus Christ.**

**Non-Christians in the world today total nearly four billion, compared to fewer than two billion Christians. So it's clear to see that the world needs Jesus.** THE POINT

**Let's take a moment to pray for these unreached people.** Lead a short prayer of your own, or invite students to take turns praying aloud for the people in the world who don't know Jesus and the missionaries who are trying to bring them the gospel.

**Say: Now let's make a list of how our own church might support foreign missions.** On a sheet of newsprint, list ideas teenagers come up with. These might include writing to church-sponsored missionaries to find out more about their needs and to learn more about their daily lives; fund raising for a particular missions project; daily prayer for a certain missionary family; and gathering supplies to send in response to a request, such as clothing, school supplies, or Bibles.

*FYI

If you can't fully darken the room by pulling down shades or turning off lights, that's OK. Candles and quiet time will still help teenagers focus on the task.

# LIFE APPLICATION

10 to 15 minutes

## POWER FROM THE SPIRIT

Have teenagers sit back down in a large circle. In the center of the circle, place a few candles, light them, and then turn out the lights in the room.

Read aloud Acts 1:8 and Ephesians 6:19. Before you read each Scripture, give a short explanation. Tell students that Acts 1:8 relates the last words Jesus spoke before ascending into heaven and Ephesians 6:19 was written by Paul while he was imprisoned in Rome. After you've read both Scriptures, **ask:**

- **How does the Holy Spirit help us bring people to Christ?**
- **How can you be sure you are speaking the truth of the gospel when you're telling others about Christ?**
- **What are some ways you can get over the fear of sharing your faith or the fear of leaving your comfort zone when doing mission work?**

**Say: Let's form trios. Each trio needs to take a Bible and read Matthew 28:18-20.** Give each person paper and a pen (or give teenagers small journal books if you have these available). After trios have read the Scripture, have them discuss the following questions. Have each person write his or her responses on a sheet of paper or in a journal.

**Ask:**

- **What is the message of Matthew 28:18-20?**
- **What kinds of talents do you have that might help you do mission work at home or elsewhere in the world?**
- **What knowledge do you have to share with someone as a missionary at home or overseas?**

**Say: As we have seen, the world needs Jesus. The power and confidence to share Jesus with the world comes from the Holy Spirit. Let's take a few minutes in silent prayer and reflection. Think about whether God might want you to do mission work and if he does, what your response will be. Thank God for the power he has given you to understand and share his Word through the Holy Spirit, and pray for guidance in sharing Christ with the world.**

THE POINT

After a few minutes, turn on the lights and blow out the candles.

**Say: Now let's make a commitment to mission work because the world needs Jesus. Discuss with your trio members what you might like to do personally to contribute to global mission work. Refer to the list we made earlier, and make a commitment on your paper. Be sure to include the specific mission you will do and the time frame in which you'll complete your mission.**

THE POINT

When teenagers have finished writing their commitments, have trio members affirm one another by encouraging one another to remember the power of the Holy Spirit as they complete their missions.

Encourage teenagers to keep journals of their mission experiences and to share mission projects with the church congregation to get other church members involved. You might also have weekly mission updates at your youth meetings, including sharing correspondence with missionaries or reporting progress on projects.

*FYI

This activity is aimed at leading teenagers to commit to individual plans of action. But if you choose, you may commit as a group to a larger-scale project. For instance, if your group has the resources to take a mission trip out of your area, this might be a good time to commit to a project such as sponsoring a missionary family or needy child, attending a workcamp in the United States (contact Group Workcamps at 1-800-774-3838), or even planning a mission trip out of the country. Take this activity as far as you want to go, and remember to rely on the power of the Holy Spirit if your teenagers choose a project that might seem too big for your group.

## OPTIONAL ACTIVITY

**10 to 15 minutes**

If you don't think your teenagers are ready to make a commitment to missions, try this optional activity instead of the "Power From the Spirit" activity.

**Say:** **Probably very few of us will actually travel elsewhere in the world to do mission work. There are many mission needs right here in our own city and state. The term "global missions" encompasses the whole world, including the people right next door. Can you help me list some ideas for mission work here at home?**

On a sheet of newsprint, list ideas as teenagers brainstorm. Ideas might include volunteering time in a soup kitchen, homeless shelter, free medical clinic, or nursing home; helping with your church's vacation Bible school or Sunday school classes; conducting clothing or food drives for needy people; adopting a child as a group through Compassion International; or committing to bring friends (especially unchurched or non-Christian teenagers) to your youth group or class.

**Ask:**
- **How can you share your faith while doing these missions?**
- **What kinds of sacrifices might you have to make to do this service for God?**

**Say:** **Now, everyone stand up—we're going to do something fun. Line up** (pause as you direct teenagers to form a single file line)**, and one by one, we're going to sing solos. Think about whether you'd rather sing "Hark, the Herald Angels Sing" or "How Great Thou Art."** Pause while teenagers grumble or voice their objections. Then **ask:**

- **Does it make you uncomfortable to think about singing a solo?**
- **How might those feelings be like the way you might feel about sharing your faith?**

**Say:** **I asked you to sing solos to give you an idea of how it feels to step out of your comfort zone. To bring people to Christ or to spread God's Word, you often have to step out of your comfort zone, almost like singing a solo in front of a crowd of people. Often we fail to share our faith with others because we fear rejection, failure, or just sounding stupid.**

**Ask:**
- **How do you motivate yourself to do something even if it makes you feel uncomfortable?**

- **How can you become comfortable doing something that was previously uncomfortable or scary?**

**Say: Often we can expand our comfort zones by practicing what we feel uncomfortable doing, by taking lessons, by learning more about a subject, or even by praying for strength and power. I won't make you sing solos today. Instead, I encourage you to consider how you can become powerful as a witness of Christ's love so that you can share him with a world that needs him.** THE POINT

*FYI

Whether your group chooses to do individual mission experiences close to home, support foreign missions, or actually plan a mission trip, there are many resources available to help you.

The Internet is full of Web sites focusing on global missions and includes directories of mission agencies, details of missionary needs, opportunities for youth mission trips, and details about unreached people.

Popular Internet search engines can point you to a variety of sites about Christian missions. Here are a couple of useful Web sites:

- **Global Mapping International**—www.gmi.org. This site is a treasure-trove of mission statistics, agencies, databases, and resources, and leads to numerous other mission Web sites.
- **Group Publishing, Inc. (Group Workcamps)**—www.grouppublishing.com. Group Publishing sponsors workcamps for teenagers throughout the country each summer.

Here are some addresses for a few of the larger mission agencies:

**Compassion International**
Colorado Springs, CO 80997
1-800-336-7676
www.compassion.com

**World Vision Inc.**
P.O. Box 9716
Federal Way, WA 98063-9716
1-888-511-6598
www.worldvision.org

**Wycliffe Bible Translators**
P.O. Box 628200
Orlando, FL 32862-8200
1-800-WYCLIFFE
www.wycliffe.org

**Campus Crusade for Christ International**
100 Lake Hart Dr.
Orlando, FL 32832
(407) 826-2000
www.campuscrusade.com

And, of course, your own denomination's headquarters can share missionary information with your group.

# TAKING UP THE CROSS

Compared to Christians in centuries past or Christians in some parts of the world today, those of us in the Western Hemisphere aren't subject to much suffering or persecution because of our faith. Yet we do sometimes suffer because of our beliefs if we imply through our words or actions that other people aren't living up to the standards Christ set for us. Our suffering may take the form of ridicule or ostracism, which is a particularly difficult prospect for teenagers who want so desperately to fit in and be liked by their peers.

If they are to be followers of Christ, it's important that teenagers be willing to stand up for what they believe, even if they have to take a little heat for doing so.

In this study, teenagers will be prompted to think about their willingness to share their beliefs when faced with possible conflict or ostracism. They'll learn why a loving God allows us to suffer and discover what the "up" side of suffering can be. Teenagers will gain an appreciation for the value of suffering when they realize that Jesus had to endure much greater suffering than they are asked to. And they'll be challenged to risk and accept suffering when it has the potential for leading others to our heavenly Father.

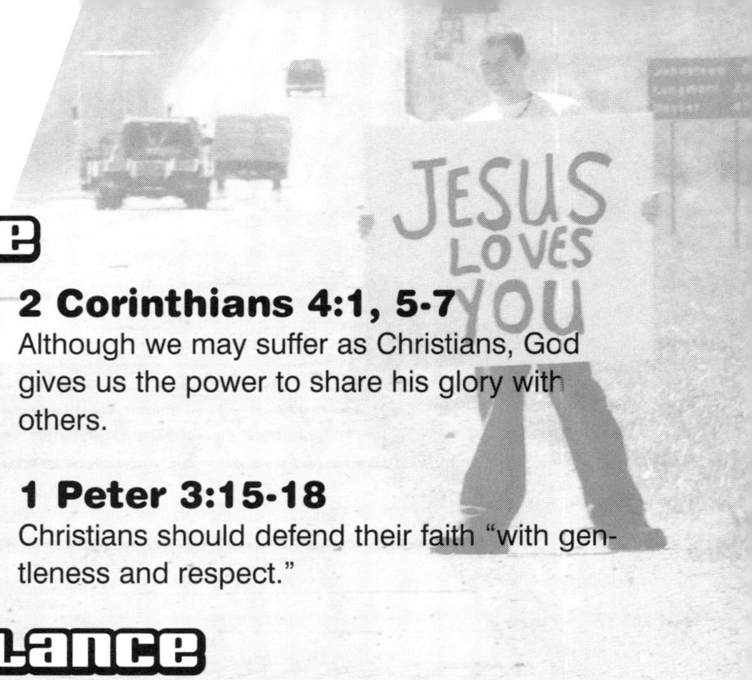


## THE POINT

**Jesus suffered for us.**

## SCRIPTURE SOURCE

### Psalm 70

The psalmist responds to suffering by crying out to God.

### Acts 5:12-42; 6:8-10; 7:51-60; 12:1-17; 16:16-34

Many members of the early church were persecuted because of their faith in Christ.

### 2 Corinthians 4:1, 5-7

Although we may suffer as Christians, God gives us the power to share his glory with others.

### 1 Peter 3:15-18

Christians should defend their faith "with gentleness and respect."

## THE STUDY AT A GLANCE

### #1 For Starters

15-20 Minutes

**■ DECISIONS, DERISIONS**

**What students will do:**
*Listen to scenarios, choose a course of action for each scenario, and think about times they took a stand (or wish they had) for their beliefs.*

SUPPLIES:
- ❑ chalkboard
- ❑ chalk
- ❑ pencils
- ❑ tape
- ❑ paper

**■ OPTIONAL ACTIVITY**
**15-20 Minutes**

**What students will do:**
*Hear and discuss real stories of Christians experiencing persecution.*

SUPPLIES:
- ❑ stories (from books, magazines, or Web sites) of Christians being persecuted

### #2 Bible Truth

20-25 Minutes

**■ ADMIRABLE ACTS**

**What students will do:**
*Examine early Christians' responses to persecution, compose and present psalms, and learn why and how we should share Christ with others even at the risk of persecution.*

SUPPLIES:
- ❑ Bibles
- ❑ "Admirable Acts" handouts (p. 46)
- ❑ pencils

### #3 Life Application

10-15 Minutes

**■ SHARING FAITH AIN'T FOR WIMPS**

**What students will do:**
*Discuss their personal experiences with suffering because of their faith and create symbols to remind them of the Christian response to persecution.*

SUPPLIES:
- ❑ Bibles
- ❑ materials such as plastic foam, paper clips, tape, paper, markers, and modeling clay
- ❑ pencils
- ❑ papers from "Decisions, Derisions" activity

## BEFORE THE STUDY

On a chalkboard or a sheet of newsprint taped to a wall in your classroom, write "A" on the top left side. Toward the top center, write "B," and on the top right side, write "C." Make sure you leave plenty of space between the three choices.

On a table, set out materials for teenagers to use to create symbols in the "Sharing Faith Ain't for Wimps" activity.

# FOR STARTERS

15 to 20 minutes

### DECISIONS, DERISIONS

After teenagers have arrived, direct them to the middle of the room and point out the three letters on the wall. Ask teenagers to listen to the following situations and decide which of the three courses of action they would most likely take in each situation. Explain that when they have made their decisions, they are to go to the board and take their places near the letters that correspond with the choices they've selected.

**Say:** **Scenario One: You are walking through the mall when you pass a group of teenagers sitting on a bench. One of them tosses a bag of fast-food trash in the potted-plant display behind him and sees you watching. You would (A) walk by, but give him a dirty look; (B) pick up the bag and put it in the nearest trash can; or (C) stop in front of him and say, "There's a garbage can right over there. If you don't want to put your trash in it, I will," then pause to see what he does.**

Wait for students to move to A, B, or C, indicating the course of action they would take. Then **say:**

**Scenario Two: You are sitting in the school cafeteria with a group of classmates, and they start talking negatively about someone in one of your classes. Although you are shocked by what you hear and doubt that it's true, the information is intriguing. You would (A) not say anything and resolve to keep the rumor to yourself; (B) tell the subject of the rumor what's being rumored; or (C) express that you don't feel right talking about people behind their backs. If the gossip continues, quietly get up and leave.**

***FYI**

Some approaches to sharing faith are more effective than others, depending on circumstances, personalities, and the depth of one's convictions. There are times a Christian feels compelled to express a belief, even if doing so results in conflict. At other times, Christian faith sharing might be more effective when a more passive approach is used. (A person who quietly makes the Christlike choice in a difficult situation can make a very strong impression.) As teenagers grapple with the choices presented in the scenarios, make sure they understand that option C is not always the *right* one to select. In fact, the appropriateness or effectiveness of choosing option C might be an interesting topic for discussion as you bring this activity to a close.

Pause while students make their choices.

**Say: Scenario Three: Your best friend, Dave, and his girlfriend, Janice, have been dating each other exclusively for several months, but on Saturday night you happen to see Janice holding hands with another guy. When you see him on Monday, Dave comments that he and Janice don't keep any secrets from each other. You would (A) not mention what you saw on Saturday night; (B) let Janice know in a roundabout way that you saw her on Saturday night; or (C) pick an appropriate place and time to ask Dave if Janice has told him about the guy you saw her with on Saturday night.**

Wait for students to make their choices.

**Say: Scenario Four: Someone in your history class got the answers to the final exam, and the list is being passed around. You would (A) refuse to look at the list, and continue studying for the exam; (B) send the teacher an anonymous note letting him or her know about the list; or (C) tell your classmates that a good grade on the exam won't mean anything if you have to cheat to get it and that you'll have to let the teacher know the answers are going around.**

Wait for students to make their choices.

**Say: Scenario Five: An English course at your school has been gaining in popularity ever since the teacher started taking her classes to the Shakespeare festival and making the field trip an overnighter. The teacher doesn't realize it, but a lot of underage drinking goes on during these field trips. Sure enough, during the trip you attend, your roommate sneaks a case of beer into your hotel room, and teenagers start filing in. You would (A) not make an issue of it; (B) call the instructor from the lobby and tell her there's a great party going on in room 313; or (C) take your roommate aside, tell him or her you feel uncomfortable with the beer in your room, and ask that the party be taken elsewhere.**

After teenagers have made their choices, **ask:**

- **Why is it hard to speak up sometimes, even when you know you're right?**
- **Which of these options (A, B, or C) would make you the most uncomfortable?**
- **If you were to choose the most uncomfortable option in each of these scenarios, what might be some *positive* outcomes?** (You might need to read

**FYI**

If teenagers have a hard time thinking of personal experiences of suffering, be prepared to tell about a time you were treated badly or felt discomfort because of your beliefs.

the scenarios and options aloud again so teenagers can come up with ideas.)

- **Do you see any similarities between the suffering that Christ endured and the suffering you might have to go through if you chose option C in any of these scenarios? Explain.**

Give each person a pencil and a sheet of paper, and **say:**

**I'd like you to take a moment to think of a time you suffered for standing firm in a particular conviction and doing what you thought was right. If you can't think of a time you spoke up (or stood firm) and consequently suffered, think instead of a time you wish you had spoken up but instead kept quiet. Write what you thought of on your sheet of paper, fold it in half, and hold on to it until later.**

**Today we're going to think and talk about suffering, especially as it pertains to living and sharing our faith. We know that Jesus suffered for us. In trying to help people understand God, it was necessary for Jesus to expose their sin, and so Jesus brought anger and suffering on himself. The people who choose to follow Christ often risk persecution because of their belief in him. Let's look at the experiences of some of Christ's followers.**

THE POINT

## OPTIONAL ACTIVITY

**15 to 20 minutes**

If your group is ready for a more sobering challenge, try this optional activity in place of the "Decisions, Derisions" activity.

Read aloud a few true stories of Christians experiencing persecution for their faith. You can obtain these stories from sources such as these:

- the book *Jesus Freaks* by DC Talk (Albury Publishing)
- *Foxe's Book of Martyrs*
- Christian History magazine
- the Web site www.christianitytoday.com/history
- the Web site www.persecution.org

After each story, ask students to discuss what you've read.

**Ask:**
- **What would you do if you were being persecuted in this way?**
- **How would such persecution affect your faith?**

After you've read all the stories, **ask:**

- **Why do you think Christians experience persecution?**
- **Why do you think God allows his people to suffer?**
- **How should we respond to persecution?**

**Say: Today we're going to think and talk about suffering for living and sharing our faith. We know that Jesus suffered for us. In trying to help people understand God, it was necessary for Jesus to expose their sin, and so Jesus brought anger and suffering on himself. The people who choose to follow Christ often risk persecution because of their belief in him. Let's look at the experiences of some of Christ's followers in the Bible.**

THE POINT

*NOTES

# BIBLE TRUTH

20 to 25 minutes

## ADMIRABLE ACTS

**Say:** **In this next activity, you're going to write a psalm. Does everyone know what a psalm is?** Make sure that teenagers understand that a psalm is a poem or a song used in worship, then read aloud Psalm 70 to give them a specific example.

**Say:** **Although this particular psalm was written many years before the earliest Christians began to be persecuted, the psalm writer was feeling in need of God's protection and strength just as persecuted Christians may feel. I'm going to ask you to take a look at some Christians who stood firm in the face of persecution. Then I want you to compose psalms on their behalf. Put yourselves in their shoes, and write psalms that sound like ones they might have written. It's OK to use modern, everyday language.**

Divide the teenagers into four groups, and number the groups from one to four. Give each group a copy of the "Admirable Acts" handout (p. 46) and a pencil. Ask each group to look up its assigned Bible passage and then compose a psalm to God written from the viewpoint of the main character or characters in the passage. Groups can write their psalms on the back of their handouts.

**Say:** **The psalms you compose should be about the characters' suffering and should communicate the answers to the questions on the handout.**

After about fifteen minutes, ask someone from each group to read the group's psalm aloud. When all of the groups have read their psalms, ask for a round of applause. Then **ask:**

- **Why do you think the Christians we read about in Acts were allowed to suffer?**
- **How did they respond to their persecution?**

Have someone read 1 Peter 3:15-18 aloud. Then **ask** the entire group:

- **What do these verses say about sharing Christ with others?**
- **Why did Jesus suffer for us?**

Read aloud 2 Corinthians 4:1, 5-7, then **ask:**

- In what ways does God give us power to withstand suffering for his name?
- According to this passage and the passage in 1 Peter, how should we respond to suffering?
- How can our response to persecution bring others to Christ?

**Say:** Whenever we are facing persecution, it's important to remember that Jesus suffered for us. His suffering was not only physical but emotional as well. The Bible says that Jesus was *rejected* by the very people he had come to save. Eventually, he was also *deserted* by those who had followed him! Jesus faced persecution to bring us into a right relationship with God, but it has also been suggested that Jesus suffered to teach *us* how to suffer. In his book, *Cry, the Beloved Country,* Alan Paton says, "I have never thought that a Christian would be free of suffering. For our Lord suffered. And I have come to believe that He suffered, not to save us from suffering, but to teach us how to bear suffering. For He knew that there is no life without suffering."

THE POINT

**Ask:**
- What do you think Jesus' life can teach us about suffering?

**Say:** You may have heard the expression that someone has "aged gracefully." Well, Jesus is someone who *suffered* gracefully. He was able to do so because he trusted in the wisdom and goodness of his heavenly Father and understood his own purpose in the world. In the hours just before he was arrested and crucified, Jesus prayed, "My Father, if it is not possible for this cup to be taken away unless I drink it, may your will be done." Jesus chose not to try to escape suffering but to suffer gracefully. You cannot escape suffering during this lifetime. But you can suffer gracefully if you understand your purpose and remember that God's opinion of you is the one that matters.

*NOTES

# LIFE APPLICATION

10 to 15 minutes

## SHARING FAITH AIN'T FOR WIMPS

**Say: Now I'd like you to look back at what you wrote on your paper at the beginning of our study. Think about what you've learned today about the reasons we suffer and the way God calls us to respond to persecution. Find a partner, and tell him or her about your personal example of suffering. If you feel you would have handled the situation differently if you had applied the advice found in the Bible passages, tell your partner what you would have done differently.**

Give pairs a few minutes to share, then have pairs reread 1 Peter 3:15-18 together.

**Say: Now I'd like each of you to use the materials I've set out to create a symbol that represents the meaning of this Scripture. Make it something that will remind you of the reason we are called to suffer for our faith and the way we should respond to persecution.** Give teenagers a few minutes to create their symbols, then ask volunteers to share their symbols with the group. Ask teenagers to bow their heads to close in prayer.

**Pray: Dear God, whenever we feel persecuted, remind us that Jesus suffered for us, and that if we, too, are willing to speak up, it is possible to bring others to you. Give us the courage to share our faith with others, even if it makes us uncomfortable. In our most difficult moments, give us the strength and confidence to suffer gracefully. In Jesus' name we pray, amen.**

THE POINT

*FYI

According to the Bible, clouds of suffering contain a number of silver linings. For example, suffering draws us to God (2 Corinthians 7:8-10); can glorify God (1 Peter 4:1-2); prepares us for joy to come (1 Peter 4:12-13); and makes us better people (James 1:2-4 and 1 Peter 5:10). The Bible also promises that God will bless those who suffer for doing good things (Matthew 5:10 and 1 Peter 3:13-14). You might want to ask teenagers to find other biblical references to the positive effects of suffering.

# ADMIRABLE ACTS

Look up the passage, answer the questions below, and use your answers to compose a psalm to God based on the character's or characters' point of view.

**Group One**—Acts 5:12-42

**Group Two**—Acts 6:8-10; 7:51-60

**Group Three**—Acts 12:1-17

**Group Four**—Acts 16:16-34

- *Who* did the suffering in this particular passage?

- *How* did that person (or persons) suffer?

- What did that person (or persons) *do* to bring on the suffering?

- How did that person (or persons) *respond* to the suffering?

# CHANGED 4 LIFE

Encourage teenagers to respond to the truth of God's Word in these studies by committing to tell their stories to others.

Ask each student to think of one person who needs to hear his or her faith story. Then challenge students to commit to sharing their stories with those people they've identified.

For those students who are ready to commit to this challenge, create a poster or banner that will hang in your meeting area. On that poster or banner, have students write the names of the people they'll share their stories with. Then ask each of those students to put his or her faith story on a separate poster or banner—either by writing the story or by illustrating it in some way. Don't hang these "story" posters or banners yet.

Once students have finished putting together their stories, challenge them to prayerfully seek opportunities to share their stories with the people they committed to.

When students have completed the challenge, encourage them to hang their individual posters or banners on the walls in your meeting area as a celebration of what God has done

JESUS LOVES YOU